1 9 8 4
The Year You Were Born

Birth Certificate

Name: _____

Birthdate: _____

Time: _____

Place of Birth: _____

Weight: _____ Length: _____

Mother's maiden name: _____

Father's name: _____

To Christopher and Scott Graham from Auntie Jeanne   J.M.

For Tallin, in bocca al lupo, Roma, 1984   J.L.

Library of Congress Cataloging in Publication Data
Martinet, Jeanne (Jeanne M.)
The year you were born, 1984/compiled by Jeanne Martinet;
illustrated by Judy Lanfredi.—1st ed.
p. cm.
Summary: Presents an assortment of events, news items,
and facts for each day of the year 1984.
ISBN 0-688-11079-7 (trade).—ISBN 0-688-11080-0 (lib. bdg.)
1. Nineteen eighty-four, A.D.—Chronology—Juvenile literature.
2. United States—History—1969—Chronology—Juvenile literature.
[1. Calendars. 2. Nineteen eighty-four, A.D.—Chronology.]
I. Lanfredi, Judy, ill. II. Title.
E876.M364 1992 031.02—dc20 91-34577 CIP AC

1 3 5 7 9 10 8 6 4 2
First edition

1 9 8 4
The Year You Were Born

Compiled by

JEANNE MARTINET

Illustrated by

JUDY LANFREDI

Tambourine Books ● New York

U.S. Almanac
1984

Year of the Olympics

Presidential election year

Leap year

United States population
237,001,000

Size of U.S.
3,618,770 square miles

President
Ronald Reagan

Largest city
New York, population 7,164,742

Biggest state (in area)
Alaska, 591,004 square miles

Number of Births in U.S.
3,669,000
Boys 1,879,000
Girls 1,790,000

Deaths in U.S.
2,046,000

Tornadoes
907

Households with television sets
83,800,000
Households with VCRs
8,880,000

Top crop
Corn
Total 1984 output
195 million metric tons

Beverages consumed
139.8 gallons per person
(including 44.2 gallons of soft drinks and 27 gallons of milk)

Children's books sold
188,000,000

Automobiles bought
14,100,000

Top movie (highest earnings)
Ghostbusters, $128,216,446

Top spectator sport
The XXIII Olympic Summer Games

Top record album
Thriller (total world sales reached $45 million)

Most popular girl's name
Jennifer
Most popular boy's name
Michael

Most rain
Little Rock, Arkansas, 63.96 inches
Most snow
Marquette, Michigan, 159.9 inches

January

January is named after Janus, the Roman god of doorways and of beginnings.

BIRTHSTONE *Garnet*

SUNDAY
January 1

New Year's Day • A powerful earthquake (7.5 on the Richter scale) rocks Japan.

MONDAY
January 2

A 9-inch, 22-pound World War II shell drops out of the sky and lands on a backyard patio in Lakewood, California, leaving a 4-foot hole. Officials are baffled.

TUESDAY
January 3

President Ronald Reagan announces that he will run for reelection. • In Farmington, Connecticut, it's the first day of the monthlong Great TV Tune-out. Some 5,000 residents have agreed to cut down their viewing, and 1,042 won't watch *any* television for at least one week!

WEDNESDAY
January 4

Wildlife officials deliver hay to hungry elk near Gunnison, Colorado, to help them survive the colder than normal winter. • Al Hamburg of Torrington, Wyoming, announces that his dog, Woofer D. Coyote, is running for president.

THURSDAY
January 5

In St. Louis, Missouri, bird-watchers have spotted a rare slaty-backed gull usually seen only in the Soviet Union. Bird enthusiasts from all over the U.S. are "flocking" to the area to catch a glimpse.

FRIDAY
January 6

The Mardi Gras festival begins in New Orleans, Louisiana. • Hitachi, Ltd., has developed a computer memory chip capable of storing over 1,000,000 characters!

SATURDAY
January 7

Prime Minister Zhao Ziyang of China arrives in Hawaii for a visit to the U.S. and Canada. It's the first time a Communist Chinese prime minister has come to America.

WHO ELSE WAS BORN IN JANUARY?
MARY LOU RETTON

Gymnast
She became the first American woman to win an
individual Olympic gold medal in gymnastics,
which she did during the 1984 Summer Olympic
Games, at age 16!
BORN January 24, 1968, in Fairmont, West
Virginia

SUNDAY
January 8

STARLING WARS: The citizens of Fairfield,
California, are trying to get rid of 10,000
starlings, which have settled uninvited in
a nearby grove of trees, by buzzing them
with remote-controlled model airplanes.

MONDAY
January 9

For the first time in 117 years, the U.S. enjoys full diplomatic
relations with the Vatican in Italy.

TUESDAY
January 10

CABBAGE PATCH CAPER: FBI agents confiscate thousands of
counterfeit Cabbage Patch dolls from a New Jersey warehouse.

WEDNESDAY
January 11

Major winter snowstorm hits the Northeast. • In Hatfield,
Massachusetts, wildlife officials are trying to decide what to do
about a bear named Frieda. Instead of hibernating, she is
roaming around town holding up traffic.

HAPPY BIRTHDAY

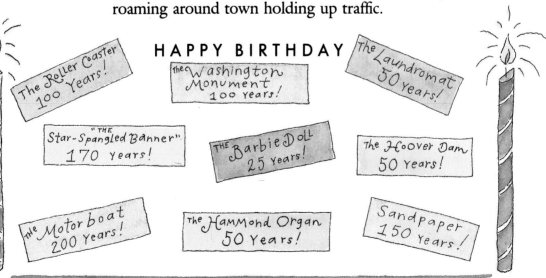

The Roller Coaster 100 Years!

The Washington Monument 100 Years!

The Laundromat 50 Years!

"THE Star-Spangled Banner" 170 Years!

THE Barbie Doll 25 Years!

The Hoover Dam 50 Years!

THE Motorboat 200 Years!

THE Hammond Organ 50 Years!

Sandpaper 150 Years!

THURSDAY
January 12

Ferocious dust storms in Helena, Montana! The city dumped a large amount of sand on top of 20 inches of snow to provide traction; but all the snow melted, and the leftover sand is now the problem.

FRIDAY
January 13

Last day of the Pennsylvania Farm Show, the largest event of its kind in the U.S. This year more than 300,000 people attend, and there are 300 exhibitors, 157 horses, 423 pigs and hogs, 624 sheep, 971 cows, and 126 goats!

SATURDAY
January 14

Tim Collum of Boyd, Texas, is crowned U.S. Video Game King in a ceremony in Ottumwa, Iowa, which calls itself the Video Game Capital of the World.

SUNDAY
January 15

Anniversary of the birth of Martin Luther King, Jr. • In Oak Ridge, Tennessee, 1,700 pounds of uranium are missing from a nuclear weapons plant. • Winthrop, Washington, holds its annual Snowshoe Softball Tournament.

MONDAY
January 16

The National Science Foundation announces its plans to drill the ocean floor in the Gulf of Mexico to study the evolution of the earth's waters.

TUESDAY
January 17

The U.S. Supreme Court rules that VCR owners may tape from television broadcasts, but only for their personal use.

WEDNESDAY
January 18

Full Moon

A crowd in Islamorada, Florida, cheers as Lucky, a 350-pound sea turtle, swims with her brand-new artificial rubber flippers for the first time! Marine experts attached them after she lost her own in a shark attack.

THURSDAY
January 19

A freezing wind from the North Pole, nicknamed the Siberian Express, engulfs two-thirds of the U.S. in temperatures 20–30 degrees below normal.

FRIDAY
January 20

It's Hat Day in elementary schools across the U.S. • In Clearwater, Florida, David Werder breaks the world record for pole-sitting: He's been sitting on a small platform at the top of a 40-foot pole for 439 days.

SATURDAY
January 21

Fifteen of the world's most famous magicians perform at the International Festival of the Magical Arts in Scottsdale, Arizona.

SUNDAY
January 22

In football's Super Bowl XVIII, the Los Angeles Raiders beat the Washington Redskins, 38-9.

FUN FACT '84

Alaska has the world's largest concentration of bald eagles, more than 3,500, as well as the most walruses and sockeye salmon.

MONDAY
January 23

Major renovation work to repair and restore the 98-year-old Statue of Liberty begins today—scaffolding is going up! Officials hope to have the statue's "face-lift" completed by her 100th birthday in 1986.

TUESDAY
January 24

Apple Computer, Inc., introduces a new personal computer to the world. It is called the Macintosh, after the inventor's favorite kind of apple.

WEDNESDAY
January 25

In the annual State of the Union address, President Reagan announces his support for the development of a permanently manned space station, which would eventually be a base for the colonization of the Moon or Mars.

THURSDAY
January 26

The U.S. Postal Service issues a commemorative stamp to mark the 100th anniversary of the birth of Harry S. Truman, the 33d president of the U.S.

FRIDAY
January 27

Michael Jackson's hair catches fire during the filming of a Pepsi-Cola commercial, after the material used to make the background smoke accidentally explodes.

SATURDAY
January 28

Leavie Cater of Santa Monica, California, has been granted a patent for a collapsible, portable cabin. It can be set up in 3 to 4 minutes.

BALD EAGLE ALERT

The bald eagle is the only eagle native to North America and has been the United States's national bird since 1782. Bald eagles are usually about 3 feet long—and have a wingspan of 7 feet! White feathers around its head and neck give the eagle a "bald" look. Bald eagles are graceful, powerful, courageous, and loyal birds. For years, they have been close to extinction and have been listed on the U.S. endangered species list.

On January 6, 1984, about 3,500 officials of the National Wildlife Federation begin a nationwide bald eagle survey to find out if the bald eagle is coming back as a species. Biologists and other scientists fly in small planes to spot the birds. They count 12,791 bald eagles, compared with 12,098 in 1983—a good sign!

SUNDAY
January 29

The Olympic torch is lit from the sun's rays at Olympia in Greece and starts its journey to Sarajevo in Yugoslavia for the Winter Games.

MONDAY
January 30

A blizzard with winds up to 60 miles per hour covers the Midwest with a thick blanket of snow. • A skiing expert reports that thumbs, not legs, are now the part of the body most likely to be injured on the slopes.

TUESDAY
January 31

They're arguing in Dallas, Texas, over the town's bunny buses ("Hop-a-Bus"), which are pink, with whiskers, buckteeth, and 3-foot-high ears. Riders like them, but city officials feel they are undignified.

ELEPHANT SEAL SUCCESS

In late January of 1984, at Año Nuevo Point in California, researchers take a count of elephant seals. The seals, which were almost extinct at the end of the 1800s, are now estimated to number 64,000!

STUDY LINKS CHOLESTEROL TO HEART DISEASE

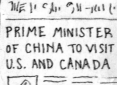
PRIME MINISTER OF CHINA TO VISIT U.S. AND CANADA

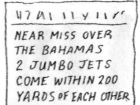
NEAR MISS OVER THE BAHAMAS 2 JUMBO JETS COME WITHIN 200 YARDS OF EACH OTHER

SEA TURTLE GETS ARTIFICIAL FLIPPERS

February

*T*he name February comes from the Latin *Februa*, which means "feast of purification."

BIRTHSTONE *Amethyst*

WEDNESDAY
February 1

To mark the beginning of Black History Month the U.S. Postal Service issues a new 20-cent stamp commemorating black historian Carter G. Woodson.

THURSDAY
February 2

Groundhog Day; also Chinese New Year, the beginning of the Year of the Rat • Frieda, the Massachusetts bear with insomnia, has been given tranquilizers and taken to an artificial den.

FRIDAY
February 3

Space shuttle *Challenger* is launched from Cape Canaveral, Florida, carrying a 5-person crew. A communications satellite, the *Westar 6*, is deployed but then disappears in space!

SATURDAY
February 4

Astronomers have announced plans to build what will be the largest telescope constructed since 1948. It will cost $7 million and be located on Sacramento Peak in New Mexico.

SUNDAY
February 5

A small earthquake at Mount St. Helens in southwest Washington makes scientists fear that the volcano is about to erupt. • A blizzard blusters through Colorado and Utah.

MONDAY
February 6

In Elmwood Park, Illinois, a week-long school cafeteria boycott ends after students' demands are met: From now on, there will be fruits and cooked vegetables in the food line, and hamburger pickles will no longer cost 5 cents extra!

TUESDAY
February 7

HUMAN SATELLITE: Astronaut Bruce McCandless floats in space up to 320 feet away from *Challenger* with no cord connecting him to the craft—the first unattached space walk in history.

WEDNESDAY
February 8

The XIV Olympic Winter Games open in Sarajevo, Yugoslavia. • Three Soviet cosmonauts are launched in a *Soyuz* space capsule. With the 5 U.S. astronauts already in orbit, there are now 8 people in space—a new record!

SOME INVENTIONS OF 1984
February 11 is National Inventors Day!

Orchard warmer
Glue gun
Bulletproof jacket for dogs
Mittens for dogs
Potato-powered clock
Electronic shoes
World's smallest organ

Wind skier
Pocket television
Paraplane
Robot bartender
Two-way mailbox
Umbrella coat
Megabit computer memory chip

THURSDAY
February 9

The Cabbage Patch Kids world expands with 2 new Cabbage Patch items: younger dolls called Preemies and animals called Koosas, which come with collars and identification tags.

FRIDAY
February 10

Space shuttle *Challenger* lands at Kennedy Space Center in Florida. • In Chicago, a 28-pound lobster named Sandy Claws II is raffled off in a charity lottery. Sandy is 105 years old!

SATURDAY
February 11

Earthquakes rock central Greece and northwestern Montana. • A blizzard leaves 3 feet of snow in Colorado, and the nation's first tornadoes of 1984 sweep through 5 states.

SUNDAY
February 12

The U.S. wins its first medal at the Olympic Winter Games: A silver goes to brother-and-sister team Caitlin and Peter Carruthers for pairs figure skating.

MONDAY
February 13

Stormie Jones, a 6-year-old girl from Texas, becomes the first person to have a simultaneous heart and liver transplant.

TUESDAY
February 14

Valentine's Day
• The Barbie doll is 25 years old today.

HAPPY BIRTHDAY TO BARBIE

In 1984, when Barbie is only 25, there are already 200,000,000 Barbie dolls in existence. It is estimated that by next year, the Barbie population could outnumber the people in the U.S.!

WHO ELSE WAS BORN IN FEBRUARY?
MICHAEL JORDAN

Basketball player, guard
Nicknamed Air Jordan, he started his professional
basketball career in 1984 with the Chicago Bulls.
Jordan also played on the gold-medal-winning
Olympic team the same year.
BORN   February 17, 1963, in Brooklyn, New
York

WEDNESDAY
February 15

At Chicago's Lincoln Park Zoo, an orangutan named Eric has given birth. Surprised zoo officials rename the new mother Erica!

THURSDAY
February 16

Full Moon

All 550 residents of Medley, Florida, are invited to put their palm prints in a new sidewalk at City Hall to be called the Sidewalk of Fame.

FRIDAY
February 17

Joe Sutorik, a scientist in Boulder, Colorado, reports a major solar flare and predicts more flares in the sun's surface during the next two weeks.

SATURDAY
February 18

There are now 5,173 man-made objects floating in space! Of these, 1,329 are orbiting satellites, and 50 are deep-space probes; the rest are "junk."

SUNDAY
February 19

The XIV Olympic Winter Games conclude. U.S. twins Phil and Steve Mahre make Olympic history by finishing first and second, respectively, in the men's slalom.

MONDAY
February 20

The National Aeronautics and Space Administration (NASA) has new evidence to suggest that every 30,000,000 years the earth is bombarded by comets and other objects, which causes mass extinction on the planet.

TUESDAY
February 21

Two clowns from California are running for president: Bozo the Clown and Wavy Gravy!

FUN FACT '84

Days are getting longer, little by little, all the time—500,000,000 years ago, a day was only 20 hours long.

WEDNESDAY
February 22

George Washington's birthday • Smidget, the world's smallest horse (21 inches tall), performs at the Midwest RV, Camping, and Travel Show in Chicago, Illinois.

THURSDAY
February 23

The American Numismatic Association, a group of coin and medal collectors and experts, meets for its midwinter convention in Colorado Springs, Colorado. • The International Boat Show takes place in Miami, Florida.

FRIDAY
February 24

SOLD OUT: The U.S. Postal Service has sold all 260,899 of the $9.35 covers ("space letters") sent into orbit with the space shuttle *Challenger* on August 30, 1983.

SATURDAY
February 25

On this day in 1951, the 22d Amendment to the Constitution was ratified, making two terms the limit for holding the office of president of the United States.

1984: CHINESE YEAR OF THE RAT
February 2, 1984–February 21, 1985

According to legend, Buddha summoned all the animals in the world to him one New Year, promising them a reward for coming. Only twelve obeyed, and he gave them each a year. The Rat arrived first, so he got the first year. (Some say he cheated and hitched a ride on the back of the Ox, jumping off in front of the Ox to be first!) The order of the 12-year cycle is always the same: Rat, Ox, Tiger, Hare, Dragon, Snake, Horse, Sheep, Monkey, Rooster, Dog, and Pig.

Rats are very charming, imaginative, and creative. They have the ability to think quickly, are honest, and seem well-equipped to deal with the "rat race." They can be nervous and aggressive, however, and sometimes have quick tempers. They get along well with Oxen and Dragons, but *not* with Hares or Horses. Famous Rats include William Shakespeare, Jimmy Carter, Julia Child, Jim Henson, Jack Spratt, and Mozart.

If you were born in 1984 before February 2, you are a Pig; but if you were born *on* or *after* February 2, you're a Rat!

LEAP YEAR

Leap years are one day longer than ordinary years because it takes the earth slightly more than 365 days to go around the sun—it actually takes 365 days, 5 hours, 48 minutes, and 46 seconds. An extra day, February 29, is added every 4 years to even things up on the calendar. Without leap year, we would eventually have Christmas in July!

Anyone born on February 29 has only one birthday every 4 years.

LEAP-YEAR BIRTHDAY CALCULATOR

Born In	Real Age (in 1992)	Leap-Year Age
1988	4	1
1984	8	2
1980	12	3
1976	16	4
1972	20	5

SUNDAY
February 26

A new card game has been invented called Raise the Roof. The object is to finish fixing up the best and biggest house in the neighborhood first!

MONDAY
February 27

Ralph Nader, the consumer activist, is 50 years old today.
• Twenty years ago, the Beatles, a rock 'n' roll group, arrived in New York City for their first American tour.

TUESDAY
February 28

During landing, a Scandinavian Airlines plane slides off the runway into Jamaica Bay at Kennedy Airport in New York City. • The 1983 Grammy Awards are presented; Michael Jackson wins for best album and best single record.

WEDNESDAY
February 29

Leap Year Day • Marsha Mann Pelekoff and Radames Pera are married aboard a DC-3 airplane before *leaping* out of the plane for their very first sky dive.

SOVIET LEADER YURI ANDROPOV DIES; KONSTANTIN CHERNENKO STEPS IN AS NEW HEAD OF USSR

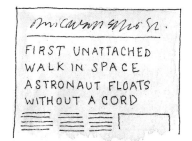

FIRST UNATTACHED WALK IN SPACE ASTRONAUT FLOATS WITHOUT A CORD

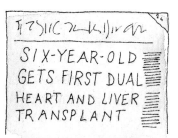

SIX-YEAR-OLD GETS FIRST DUAL HEART AND LIVER TRANSPLANT

March

*M*arch is named for the Roman god of war, Mars.

BIRTHSTONE *Aquamarine*

THURSDAY
March 1

A group of hikers in Point Conception, California, begins an 8,000-mile Walk for Peace, scheduled to end in Moscow on October 15, 1985.

FRIDAY
March 2

Today the moon is farther away from the earth than it has been at any previous time this century. • Rattlesnake Rodeo is held in Opp, Alabama.

SATURDAY
March 3

Hawaii's Kilauea volcano erupts, spewing lava 1,000 feet in the air. • In San Diego, California, 400 kites compete in the 36th annual Ocean Beach Kite Festival.

SUNDAY
March 4

U.S. Olympic gold medalist Bill Johnson wins the World Cup for downhill skiing at Aspen, Colorado, beating Austria's Helmut Hoeflehner by 25 hundredths of a second!

MONDAY
March 5

The American Kennel Club reports that the cocker spaniel has replaced the poodle as America's top dog.

TUESDAY
March 6

A 17-year-old, Louise Fitzgerald, wins the 35th annual International Pancake Race in Liberal, Kansas.

WEDNESDAY
March 7

It's Mosquito Awareness Week in Williston, North Dakota!

THURSDAY
March 8

An 11-year-old, Trevor Ferrell, of Gladwyne, Pennsylvania, is honored at a luncheon, with city officials and street people. He has brought blankets to the homeless almost every day since December.

FRIDAY
March 9

STOP THE PRESS! In honor of the 72d anniversary of the Girl Scouts of America on March 12, President Reagan lunches with Girl Scouts at the White House. Reporters are barred from the affair.

SATURDAY
March 10

HAPPY PHONE-IVERSARY: On this day in 1876, Alexander Graham Bell transmitted the first telephone message to his assistant in the next room: "Mr. Watson, come here. I want you."

SUNDAY
March 11

It's Johnny Appleseed Day. • It's also the beginning of Camp Fire Birthday Week and Fun Mail Week.

MONDAY
March 12

Wearing single white gloves, studded belts, and unlaced sneakers, 55 students crash the school board meeting at Bound Brook High School in Bound Brook, New Jersey, to protest a recently imposed ban on dressing like Michael Jackson in school.

── FUN FACT '84 ──────────

In Gulfport, Florida, Andy and Dandy Safko grow and sell 1,500,000 four-leaf clovers a year.

TUESDAY
March 13

The first fully portable cellular telephone is introduced to the public.

WEDNESDAY
March 14

One of the worst snowstorms to hit northern New England in this century leaves up to 3 feet of snow from New York to Maine. The U.S. Postal Service cancels regular deliveries in southern Maine.

THURSDAY
March 15

Scientists from Woods Hole Oceanographic Institution have discovered a community of giant clams, tube worms, and other exotic creatures in the Gulf of Mexico west of Florida.

FRIDAY
March 16

State prison officials in Florence, Arizona, have come up with a new punishment for inmates who misbehave: They get meat loaf at every meal for a whole week!

SATURDAY
March 17

Full Moon

St. Patrick's Day. Chicago turns its river green for the day, New York City paints a green stripe up Fifth Avenue, and the entire country buys green flowers.

SUNDAY
March 18

March 18 to 24 is National Wildlife Week, and Kermit the Frog has been made chairman. • There are ice storms in Kansas and Missouri, blizzards in Nebraska and Utah, and avalanches in Colorado!

MONDAY *March 19*	On this day for the past 207 years, swallows have returned from their winter home in Argentina to the town of San Juan Capistrano in California. They leave for Argentina every year on October 23.
TUESDAY *March 20*	Spring equinox • The American wood stork is added to the U.S. Fish and Wildlife Service's list of endangered species. • A major earthquake in the Soviet Union affects a 500-mile area.
WEDNESDAY *March 21*	In Montpelier, Vermont, 13-year-old Mark Bates wins the 8th annual Rotten Sneaker Contest. The prize: a new pair of sneakers.
THURSDAY *March 22*	*USA Today* reports that more than 3,000 of the nation's 10,000 video game arcades have closed in the past 9 months.
FRIDAY *March 23*	Scott Hamilton wins the men's singles title in the World Figure Skating Championships held in Ottawa, Canada.

TOP-10 SINGLES OF 1984*

1. "Owner of a Lonely Heart" — Yes
2. "Karma Chameleon" — Culture Club
3. "Jump" — Van Halen
4. "Footloose" — Kenny Loggins
5. "Against All Odds (Take a Look at Me Now)" — Phil Collins
6. "Hello" — Lionel Richie
7. "Let's Hear It for the Boy" — Deniece Williams
8. "Time After Time" — Cyndi Lauper
9. "The Reflex" — Duran Duran
10. "When Doves Cry" — Prince

Source: Billboard

SATURDAY *March 24*	Four armed men break into Brink's security vault outside Rome and make off with $22 million, the largest sum ever stolen in Italy!
SUNDAY *March 25*	U.S. scientists begin a 7-day study of the comet Crommelin, which approaches the sun every 27 years. • In Hawaii, Mauna Loa, the world's largest active volcano, erupts for the first time in almost 9 years.

WHO ELSE WAS BORN IN MARCH?
ALEXANDER GRAHAM BELL

American inventor
He was the first to patent and commercialize the telephone.
BORN March 3, 1847, in Edinburgh, Scotland

MONDAY
March 26

Eight children from 8 to 12 years old have been appointed to a new Board of Children Advisory Committee at Children's Hospital in Milwaukee, Wisconsin. They will advise the hospital on meals, visiting hours, and anything else they think important.

TUESDAY
March 27

A Piedmont Aviation jet on its way from Charleston, South Carolina, to Miami, Florida, is hijacked to Cuba.

WEDNESDAY
March 28

MONSTER STORM SYSTEM: In one of the worst storms in recent history, 24 tornadoes tear through the Carolinas and Georgia, causing more than $100 million in damage.

THURSDAY
March 29

The Maltese freighter *Eldia* runs aground at Cape Cod. Looming 3 stories high, it immediately becomes a major tourist attraction!

FRIDAY
March 30

The new Children's Zoo at the Bronx Zoo in New York City opens; there is a spiderweb for climbing and fake fox ears for listening to sounds. • In Hawaii, Kilauea and Mauna Loa are erupting together for the first time since 1868.

SATURDAY
March 31

Today is Bunsen Burner Day, honoring inventor Robert Wilhelm Eberhard Bunsen, born on this day in 1811.

SCIENTISTS WARN OF GREENHOUSE EFFECT

PRESIDENT REAGAN LUNCHES WITH GIRL SCOUTS

MAJOR DRUG BUST IN COLOMBIA

LARGEST THEFT IN ITALY $22 MILLION

April

The name April comes from the Latin *aperire*, which means "to open." Also known as the time of budding.

BIRTHSTONE *Diamond*

SUNDAY
April 1

April Fools' Day • The NCAA Women's Basketball Championship is won by the University of Southern California, which defeats Tennessee, 72-61.

MONDAY
April 2

The Mattel toy company has developed a new type of plastic that will show up on X rays, in case a toy or part of a toy has been swallowed. • Georgetown University beats Houston 84-75 to win the NCAA Men's Basketball Championship.

TUESDAY
April 3

FIRST INDIAN SPACEMAN: Along with 2 Soviet cosmonauts, Rakesh Sharma, India's first astronaut, is launched in a *Soyuz 11* capsule from central Asia.

WEDNESDAY
April 4

FBI agents arrest former army employee Richard Craig Smith as a double agent.

THURSDAY
April 5

BASKETBALL RECORD: Kareem Abdul-Jabbar of the Los Angeles Lakers becomes basketball's leading scorer during a game against the Utah Jazz. He has racked up 31,421 career points!

FRIDAY
April 6

Space shuttle *Challenger*, with a 5-man crew, lifts off from Cape Canaveral, Florida. Also on board, more than 3,300 honeybees.

SATURDAY
April 7

Jack Morris of the Detroit Tigers pitches a no-hitter against the Chicago White Sox, the first for a Detroit pitcher since 1958.

SUNDAY
April 8

U.S. astronaut George Nelson walks in space, with a rocket-powered backpack, from the *Challenger* to *Solar Max*, a satellite whose job it is to study the surface of the sun.

WHO ELSE WAS BORN IN APRIL?
HANS CHRISTIAN ANDERSEN

Fairy-tale writer, poet, and novelist
He wrote 168 fairy tales between the years 1835 and 1845.
BORN   April 2, 1805, in Odense, Denmark

MONDAY
April 9

Twenty men set out from Spetsai, Greece, on a voyage aboard a 52-foot wooden boat. They will recreate Jason and the Argonauts' mythical quest for the Golden Fleece.

TUESDAY
April 10

REPAIRMEN IN SPACE: The *Challenger* crew brings *Solar Max* into the space shuttle's cargo bay and makes repairs.

WEDNESDAY
April 11

A starving giant panda staggers into a peasant's house in China's Szechwan Province and is saved after it is taken to a special government center.

THURSDAY
April 12

Cop-of-the-month award for bravery in New York goes to a one-armed robot called RM13!

THE TORNADOES OF 1984

A tornado is the most violent kind of storm. It is a funnel-shaped, intense whirlwind, usually between one and 550 yards in diameter, that develops from severe thunderstorms. Tornadoes can destroy anyone or anything in their path.

The U.S. is the most tornado-prone country in the world. It is the only country besides Bangladesh that has twisters with winds of 200 miles per hour. Tornado season is usually March through August, and the peak tornado months are May and June.

The year 1984 was one of extreme tornado activity. There were 907 tornadoes reported. The National Weather Service had to issue a severe thunderstorm or tornado watch on almost every day during this period. Total number of tornado days: 166!

MAJOR U.S. TORNADOES IN 1984

March 28	North Carolina, South Carolina, and Georgia
April 21–22	Mississippi
April 27	From Oklahoma to Minnesota
June 7	From Wisconsin to Iowa

FRIDAY
April 13

RECORD: Baseball player Pete Rose becomes the 2d player in history to reach 4,000 hits in his career! • Space shuttle *Challenger* lands safely at Edwards Air Force base in California.

SATURDAY
April 14

An earthquake strikes eastern Austria.

SUNDAY
April 15

Full Moon

Palm Sunday • Ben Crenshaw wins the Masters Golf Tournament, beating Tom Watson by 2 strokes.

MONDAY
April 16

The 88th Boston Marathon is won by Geoff Smith of Great Britain, with a time of 2 hours, 10 minutes, and 34 seconds. The women's winner is Lorraine Moller of New Zealand.

TUESDAY
April 17

The Jewish holiday of Passover begins. • Today is the last day to go to the International Personal Robot Congress and Exposition in Albuquerque, New Mexico.

WEDNESDAY
April 18

In France, daredevils Mike MacCarthy and Amanda Tucker parachute off the Eiffel Tower.

THURSDAY
April 19

A baby girl named Cherilynn McNutt has been born in Loveland, Colorado—with 2 front teeth!

FRIDAY
April 20

To protest the placing of nuclear missiles in Western Europe, 20,000 people form a human chain around the U.S. Army base in Mutlangen, West Germany.

SATURDAY
April 21

Tornadoes whip through Mississippi.

SUNDAY
April 22

Easter. In Homer, Georgia, 40,000 eggs are boiled, colored, and hidden throughout 40 acres on Herbert Garrison's farm. They are still warm when they are found!

MONDAY
April 23

Egg Salad Week, dedicated to delicious uses for all the Easter eggs that have been cooked, colored, hidden, and found.

FUN FACT '84

The traffic light was invented by a man named Lester Farnsworth, who got the idea while reading the Bible!

TUESDAY
April 24

A powerful earthquake in California causes skyscrapers to sway in San Francisco. • Sesame Street's Bert and Ernie are kidnapped from a shopping mall in Norfolk, Virginia!

WEDNESDAY
April 25

A baby eaglet has been born at the Cleveland Museum of Natural History in Ohio. It is the only eagle to be hatched from an artificially inseminated egg. • Bert and Ernie are returned, safe and sound.

THURSDAY
April 26

Samantha Smith, the 12-year-old girl from Maine who was invited to the Soviet Union in 1983 by Yuri Andropov, has signed a contract to write a book about her experience.

FRIDAY
April 27

Earth Day • President Reagan arrives in Peking for a historic 6-day visit to China. • A blizzard in the northern Rocky Mountains sets off more than 40 tornadoes.

SATURDAY
April 28

The National Zoo in Washington, D.C., has decided to build an exercise gym for their giant pandas, Ling-Ling and Hsing-Hsing.

RAINING CATS AND DOGS

Throughout history there have been reports of tornadoes that "rain" strange things, such as frogs, fish, rats, lizards, and stones. These tales could be fibs, but tornadoes are powerful enough to suck things up from one place and set them down in another. In 1978, a number of geese were pulled into a tornado and were later dropped out of the clouds in a line stretching for 28 miles!

SUNDAY
April 29

THERE'S NO PLACE LIKE HOME: The Philadelphia Zoo's rare green macaw, Tyrone, who flew away when zoo workers didn't clip his wings properly, is found back in the zoo today!

MONDAY
April 30

The U.S. Postal Service issues a 13-cent postal card honoring the traditional carrying of the Olympic torch at the start of every Olympics.

FBI ARRESTS ARMY EMPLOYEE AS DOUBLE AGENT

FIRST INDIAN ASTRONAUT IN SPACE

PRESIDENT REAGAN VISITS CHINA FOR FIRST TIME

May

*M*ay comes from Maia, who was the Roman goddess of growth, increase, and blossoming.

BIRTHSTONE *Emerald*

TUESDAY
May 1

A Michael Jackson look-alike contest in Concord, New Hampshire, is canceled when an overwhelming 6,000 contestants show up!

WEDNESDAY
May 2

President Reagan and Pope John Paul II meet for the first time on American soil in Fairbanks, Alaska.

THURSDAY
May 3

A tornado hits Montgomery, Alabama, and neighboring areas.

FRIDAY
May 4

W. C. Gurly of Marietta, Ohio, took the first photograph of lightning 100 years ago. • The summer's big-budget film ($25 million), *The Bounty*, opens in theaters across the nation.

SATURDAY
May 5

The 110th Kentucky Derby is won by Swale. • Michael Jackson presents his mother with a Rolls Royce—tied with a big white bow—for her birthday.

SUNDAY
May 6

Because of the damage caused by tornadoes this year, weather experts are using TOTO, a transportable tornado observatory, to study why and how they happen.

MONDAY
May 7

The Olympic torch is lit from the flame burning at Olympia, Greece, and starts on its long journey to Los Angeles for the XXIII Olympic Summer Games!

TUESDAY
May 8

Runners at the United Nations in New York City start the Olympic torch on a 9,000-mile relay across the country. • The Soviet Union announces it will not participate in this summer's Olympic games.

WEDNESDAY
May 9

Big Crinkly, a 24-foot-high mobile by Alexander Calder, is sold at auction for $852,000, a new record for a sculpture by an American.

THURSDAY *May 10*	The Tennessee River in Chattanooga, Tennessee, is overflowing after 3 days of storms cause the worst river flooding in the U.S. since 1973.
FRIDAY *May 11*	The U.S. Postal Service issues a commemorative stamp for the 1984 World's Fair (the Louisiana World Exposition).
SATURDAY *May 12*	The World's Fair opens in New Orleans, Louisiana. The fair cost $350 million and has taken 10 years to plan.
SUNDAY *May 13* 	Mother's Day • Vera Komarkova from Colorado and Margita Dina Sterbova from Czechoslovakia become the first women ever to reach the top of Cho Oyu in the Himalayas, one of the world's highest mountains (26,867 feet).
MONDAY *May 14*	Mount St. Helens shoots ash and steam 4 miles into the air.
TUESDAY *May 15* Full Moon	In one of the major archaeological finds of the century, scientists discover an undamaged Mayan tomb more than 1,500 years old. Inside is a skeleton surrounded by 15 intact vessels—one with what may be the world's first screw-on top!

THAT'S SHOW BUG-NESS!

During the making of the 1984 hit adventure movie *Indiana Jones and the Temple of Doom*, director Steven Spielberg wanted to make sure there were lots of bugs crawling on the floor of the cave where he was filming. A Hollywood "bug broker" was hired to provide 50,000 crickets and 5,000 cockroaches!

WEDNESDAY *May 16*	The president of Mexico, Miguel de la Madrid Hurtado, visits the U.S.
THURSDAY *May 17*	HORSE GIVES BIRTH TO ZEBRA! Born from a zebra embryo implanted in a horse, the baby zebra is part of a national program to save endangered species from extinction.
FRIDAY *May 18*	It's Rooster Day in Broken Arrow, Oklahoma. The celebration includes a Miss Chick contest, a parade, and a 3-day rodeo.

WHO ELSE WAS BORN IN MAY?
FLORENCE NIGHTINGALE

Nurse, hospital reformer, and philanthropist
She was the founder of modern nursing and the
first woman to receive the British Order of Merit.
BORN   May 12, 1820, in Florence, Italy

SATURDAY
May 19

The Edmonton Oilers win the National Hockey League's
Stanley Cup, defeating the New York Islanders, 4 games to 1.
• In horse racing, the Preakness Stakes is won by Gate Dancer.

SUNDAY
May 20

A 300-year-old manuscript found smoldering in a garbage heap
in England has been sold at auction by Christie's in New York
City for $110,000!

MONDAY
May 21

In Angels Camp, California, Weird Harold, a frog from
Oregon, wins the Calaveras County Jumping Frog
Contest with a mighty leap of 21 feet 1½ inches.

TUESDAY
May 22

An earthquake shakes eastern China. • The Fashion
Foundation of America has named President Reagan Best-
dressed Statesman.

WEDNESDAY
May 23

New Jersey students from kindergarten through
eighth grade compete throughout the state for
best invention. Two of the winning ideas: a 2-
way mailbox and an umbrella coat.

THURSDAY
May 24

Shenandoah Spring Festival in Shenandoah, Virginia • Queen
Victoria, for whom the Victorian Age was named, was born on
this date in 1819.

FRIDAY
May 25

Six thousand farmers in northwestern Indonesia flee as Soputan
volcano erupts with a roar. • In the U.S., Mount St. Helens
rumbles.

SATURDAY
May 26

In Philadelphia, Pennsylvania, Don Cain sets a new Frisbee
record with a throw that keeps the disk in the air for 16.72
seconds.

FUN FACT '84

There are more than 30,000 different kinds of spiders in the world.

1984 AWARDS BOARD

Nobel Peace Prize: Bishop Desmond Tutu
National Teacher of the Year: Sherleen Sisney
National Spelling Bee Champion: Daniel Greenblatt
Best Movie of 1984 (Academy Award): *Amadeus*
Best Special Visual Effects (Academy Award):
   Indiana Jones and the Temple of Doom
Grammy Award (Best Album): "Can't Slow Down," Lionel Richie
Grammy Award (Best Single): "What's Love Got to Do with It,"
   Tina Turner
Male Athlete of the Year: Carl Lewis, track and field
Female Athlete of the Year: Mary Lou Retton, gymnastics
1984 Newbery Medal for Children's Literature: *Dear Mr. Henshaw* by
   Beverly Cleary

SUNDAY
May 27

TWO-TIME CHAMP: Rick Mears, who won the Indianapolis 500 in 1979, wins the race again, with an average speed of 163.621 miles per hour.

MONDAY
May 28

Memorial Day • A mule named Mrs. Reese beats 30 other mules in the annual Bay Mule Mile, an uphill race in Bend, Oregon. Meanwhile, Nosy the Mule sells kisses at the mule-kissing booth for $5 each!

TUESDAY
May 29

The Statue of Liberty is officially closed for renovation. It will not reopen until July 4, 1986.

WEDNESDAY
May 30

Scientists report the discovery of an effective chicken-pox vaccine. • Millions view a rare and dramatic "diamond necklace" annular eclipse of the sun, visible in much of the U.S.

THURSDAY
May 31

Thirteen-year-old Daniel Greenblatt of Sterling, Virginia, wins the 57th National Spelling Bee. Winning word: *luge*, a racing sled.

UNDAMAGED 1,500-YEAR-OLD MAYAN TOMB DISCOVERED

SOVIETS SAY THEY WILL BOYCOTT LOS ANGELES OLYMPICS

HAUNTED CASTLE AT NEW JERSEY AMUSEMENT PARK BURNS DOWN

June

*J*une is named for the Latin *juniores*, meaning "youths," or from the Roman goddess Juno.

BIRTHSTONE *Pearl*

FRIDAY
June 1

Donut Day in Chicago, Illinois • *Star Trek III: The Search for Spock*, the 3d movie in the Star Trek series, opens across the U.S.

SATURDAY
June 2

Ninety yachts leave Plymouth in England for Newport, Rhode Island, at the start of the Trans-Atlantic Single-handed Race.

SUNDAY
June 3

Atari, Inc., introduces its Mindlink system, which enables video-game players to manipulate objects on the screen without using their hands. Players wear headbands containing sensors and then just move their eyes or eyebrows!

MONDAY
June 4

University of California scientists have succeeded in cloning cells from the 140-year-old preserved skin of a quagga, an animal related to the horse and zebra. Quaggas have been extinct for about a century.

TUESDAY
June 5

Researchers at Los Alamos National Laboratory in New Mexico announce the development of a plastic that can conduct electricity as well as metal can.

WEDNESDAY
June 6

Americans have bought close to 2,300,000 VCRs since January 1!

THURSDAY
June 7

A violent twister levels the town of Barneveld, Wisconsin; and the state of Iowa reports a record 26 tornadoes.

FRIDAY
June 8

Nancy Reagan visits the London Zoo in England and meets her namesake: Nancy, a 2-week-old reindeer. • Back in the U.S., the tornado count for the storm system in the Midwest is 50!

SATURDAY
June 9

Donald Duck celebrates his 50th birthday. He is made an honorary marine; then marches down Disneyland's Main Street, USA, in a ticker-tape parade.

WHO ELSE WAS BORN IN JUNE?
PAUL McCARTNEY

British musician, songwriter
He became famous as a member of the Beatles
and remains a best-selling recording artist/
composer.
BORN   June 18, 1942, in Liverpool, England

SUNDAY
June 10

At the San Diego Zoo in California, a 6-ounce condor named
Pismo is born. It's the 8th California condor hatched in
captivity this year in the Condor Recovery Program.

MONDAY
June 11

An earthquake rattles central California.

TUESDAY
June 12

NICE CATCH: In Portland, Maine, Cynthia Nevers
dashes across the street and leaps over a fence to catch
a 17-month-old toddler who is falling from a 2d-floor
railing. The child is unharmed!

WEDNESDAY
June 13
Full Moon

In New York City, horse-drawn carriages are taken off the
street at noon to protect the overheated horses when
temperature records are broken thoughout the Northeast.

THURSDAY
June 14

Boston's mayor, former Celtics player Raymond L. Flynn,
proclaims Boston to be the Capital of Basketball, in honor of
the Boston Celtics winning the NBA championship on June
12. More than 200,000 fans celebrate at a parade and rally.

JACKSONMANIA

Michael Jackson breaks all records for popularity in 1984. At the
Grammy Awards in February, he wins a record 8 awards, and his
best-selling album *Thriller* is selling at the unbelievable rate of
1,000,000 copies a week! Youths throughout America wear one
white glove, a studded belt, and unlaced sneakers to try to look
like Michael Jackson. The singer's famous "moonwalk" becomes
an art form.

FRIDAY
June 15

Smile Power Day reminds everyone how important smiling is!

SATURDAY
June 16

Today is the 100th anniversary of the first American roller coaster, built at Coney Island in Brooklyn. • The International Games for the Disabled begin in Nassau County, New York, with 1,500 competitors from more than 50 countries.

SUNDAY
June 17

Father's Day • In a promotion sponsored by baseball's Baltimore Orioles, Ann Sommers wins $1 million when Gary Roenicke hits a grand-slam home run during a lucky inning.

MONDAY
June 18

Fuzzy Zoeller wins the U.S. Open golf tournament with a score of 67, the lowest play-off score in Open history.

TUESDAY
June 19

A Soviet submarine is trapped for 3½ hours in fishing wire in the North Sea, 5 miles from Norway.

WEDNESDAY
June 20

The Motion Picture Association of America has instituted a new rating for films, PG-13. This means that children under 13 cannot attend without a guardian.

THURSDAY
June 21

Summer solstice • The largest single New York Stock Exchange transaction takes place: 10,000,000 shares of Superior Oil for $423,800,000. • President and Mrs. Reagan hold an outdoor fish fry at the Congressional Seafood Festival on the South Lawn.

FUN FACT '84

There are 16,901 movie theaters in the U.S.

FRIDAY
June 22

A method for sculpting an individual's face in chocolate has been patented by Dr. Victor Syrmis. He's calling it Chocolate Photos.

SATURDAY
June 23

A guitar that once belonged to the late John Lennon, former Beatle, is sold in an auction of his belongings—for $19,000!

SUNDAY *June 24*	Arnold Palmer, age 54, wins his 87th golf tournament at the Senior Tournament Players Championship in Cleveland, Ohio.
MONDAY *June 25*	The launch of the space shuttle *Discovery* is postponed 30 minutes before liftoff, due to a computer failure.
TUESDAY *June 26*	A malfunctioning valve causes the launching of *Discovery* to be delayed again—4 seconds before liftoff!
WEDNESDAY *June 27*	**WHAT A WHEELIE:** At the Alabama International Speedway in Talladega, Alabama, Doug Domokos rides for 145 miles nonstop on the rear wheel of his motorcycle, a Honda XR 500.
THURSDAY *June 28*	Watermelon Thump in Luling, Texas, featuring watermelon judging, eating, and seed spitting.
FRIDAY *June 29*	The Soviet Union offers to begin talks with the U.S. on banning weapons in space.
SATURDAY *June 30*	The World Championship Inner Tube Race—an 8-mile float down the Colorado River—is held in Yuma, Arizona.

DOING THE BREAK

The biggest craze of 1984: break dancing, an acrobatic mixture of gymnastics, ballet, martial arts, and pantomime. Break dancers perform on sidewalks, on stages, or in shopping malls, and they often do handstands, headstands, and somersaults. Part of "the break" is balancing the body on the hands as the dancer spins. Here are some break-dancing moves:

- Moonwalk: Walk forward while sliding backward
- Popping: Dance quickly like a jerky robot
- Headwalk: Slide across the floor upside down
- Dolphin: Pretend to be a flopping fish

CAT SURVIVES FALL FROM A NEW YORK SKYSCRAPER WITH A FEW CUTS & BRUISES

SWALE, KENTUCKY DERBY WINNER, DROPS DEAD

GENES FROM EXTINCT QUAGGA REPRODUCED

50 TORNADOES RIP THROUGH MIDWEST

July

This month was named to honor Julius Caesar.

BIRTHSTONE *Ruby*

SUNDAY
July 1

In Liechtenstein, women win the right to vote.

MONDAY
July 2

CAMP FOR DOLLS: It's opening day at Camp Small Fry, a summer camp for Cabbage Patch Kids in Red Bank, New Jersey.

TUESDAY
July 3

In Arlington, Texas, postman Jeff Robbins drops his mailbag, jumps into a swimming pool, and rescues a woman who is trapped inside her car underwater!

WEDNESDAY
July 4

Independence Day • Two white tiger cubs have been born at the Henry Doorly Zoo in Omaha, Nebraska, bringing the number of these rare animals in this zoo to 6.

THURSDAY
July 5

The Statue of Liberty loses her torch! It's removed today as part of the statue's overhaul.

FRIDAY
July 6

Michael Jackson's 13-city "Victory" tour with the Jackson Brothers is launched in Kansas City, Missouri.

SATURDAY
July 7

Martina Navratilova wins her 5th Wimbledon tennis championship in women's singles, defeating Chris Evert Lloyd. The two women have faced each other on the court 60 times; they've each won 30!

SUNDAY
July 8

John McEnroe trounces Jimmy Connors in the Wimbledon tennis championships (men's singles). • There's a mild earthquake in Long Beach, California.

MONDAY
July 9

The Muppets Take Manhattan, the 3d in the Muppet film series, opens this week in movie theaters across the country.

TUESDAY
July 10

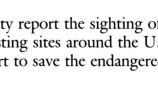

Researchers at Cornell University report the sighting of 21 pairs of peregrine falcons at nesting sites around the U.S., indicating that the 10-year effort to save the endangered species is succeeding.

WHO ELSE WAS BORN IN JULY?
AMELIA EARHART

Pioneer in aviation
In 1932, she became the first woman to fly solo across the Atlantic. In 1937, she disappeared over the Pacific Ocean on an attempted around-the-world flight.
BORN July 24, 1898, in Atchison, Kansas

WEDNESDAY
July 11

The first seat-belt law in the country is passed in New York. • Two cleaning women recover an $80,000 ring left on a plane.

THURSDAY
July 12
Full Moon

Democratic presidential candidate Walter Mondale announces that Representative Geraldine Ferraro of New York will be his running mate.

FRIDAY
July 13

Derek Fowler of Great Britain sets out from Kitty Hawk, North Carolina, to fly across the country to Lake Elsinore, California, in a microlight (a plane no heavier than 331 pounds).

SATURDAY
July 14

Ten bald eagles, a gift from Canada, are on their way to New Jersey, part of the state's 1984 eagle-replenishing program.

SUNDAY
July 15

The U.S. Women's Open golf tournament is won by Hollis Stacy—by one stroke. • 7-year-old Cari Ann Hayer wins the logrolling championship in Hayward, Wisconsin.

MONDAY
July 16

Pope John Paul II goes skiing in the Italian Alps. • In San Diego, California, TSAR (Trans-American Solar-Powered Auto Run), a car powered entirely by the sun's rays, begins a historic 2,400-mile journey to Florida.

WHAT'S HOT IN 1984

Robots	Transformers	Hair mousse	*Still* Hot:
CDs	Break dancing	Unlaced sneakers	Cabbage Patch dolls
Tofutti	Day-Glo socks	*Ghostbusters*	Michael Jackson
Prince	Barbie dolls	Macintosh computers	Trivial Pursuit

SEA MAIL

In July 1984, 13-year-old Wayne Broderick, Jr., of South Portland, Maine, received a reply to a letter he had put inside a bottle and thrown into the Atlantic Ocean in 1982. The bottle had drifted 2,500 miles before it reached the Azores, islands west of Portugal.

TUESDAY
July 17

A Soviet spacecraft, *Soyuz T-12*, is launched to link up with an orbiting space station, *Salyut 7*. On board: 2 men, 1 woman, and 1 stowaway fly!

WEDNESDAY
July 18

WORKERS ARE GETTING ANTSY: At City Hall in Trenton, New Jersey, ants are swarming over workers' desks and crawling up their legs.

THURSDAY
July 19

The Democrats officially nominate Walter Mondale to run for president and Geraldine Ferraro to run for vice president—the first woman vice-presidential candidate in U.S. history.

FRIDAY
July 20

A brilliant white flash followed by a lingering smoke trail is seen by people from Medford, Oregon, to Ukiah, California, as well as by several airplane pilots. No traces of the strange "fiery object" are found.

SATURDAY
July 21

A huge school of anchovies swims into the harbor in Santa Cruz, California, making the water totally black!

SUNDAY
July 22

Publisher Malcolm Forbes has a rough landing when his Egyptian-sphinx-shaped balloon deflates unexpectedly during a balloon race in Reading Township, New Jersey.

MONDAY
July 23

Cleanup crews are working hard to remove 400 tons of dead anchovies from the harbor in Santa Cruz, California.

TUESDAY
July 24

The nation's largest manufacturer of electric fences announces it will change the color of its fences from red to black. Hummingbirds confused the red fences with flowers and were being electrocuted trying to get nectar.

FUN FACT '84

There are more than 100,000 shipwrecks in U.S. waters from before the year 1900.

WELCOME TO THE LOS ANGELES OLYMPICS

The Olympic Flame arrives in Los Angeles and is carried to the stadium by Gina Hemphill, the granddaughter of U.S. athlete Jesse Owens. 3,636 relay runners have brought the Flame across the country from New York City, where it arrived from Greece. At the opening ceremonies, a 1,000-voice choir sings a WELCOME, and an 800-piece band—with 84 grand pianos—plays. A Rocket Man with WELCOME on his back flies down and lands in the stadium. Five airplanes write WELCOME in huge letters in the sky.

WEDNESDAY
July 25

Svetlana Savitskaya of the U.S.S.R. becomes the first woman to walk in space. She is outside the *Salyut 7* for 3 hours, 35 minutes, and does some welding on the outside of the spacecraft.

THURSDAY
July 26

Treasure hunter Barry Clifford, aided by a British mapmaker, has found a sunken pirate ship named the *Whidah*, which sank off Cape Cod in 1717. Experts estimate the ship's artifacts to be worth $400 million.

FRIDAY
July 27

A new imaging system called the 4Shooter begins to operate, making the 200-inch reflecting telescope at the top of Palomar Mountain in California the most powerful in the world.

SATURDAY
July 28

The XXIII Olympic Summer Games open in Los Angeles.
• Scientists working off the coast of Oregon have discovered unusual marine life a mile below the surface of the Pacific, including 5-foot-long worms with red heads!

SUNDAY
July 29

Steve Lundquist sets an Olympic record when he wins the 100-meter breaststroke in 1 minute, 1.65 seconds.

MONDAY
July 30

Deep-sea explorers announce that they have found a 200-year-old British shipwreck, the *De Braak*, near Lewis, Delaware, loaded with booty captured from the Spanish in 1789.

TUESDAY
July 31

The U.S. men's team wins a gold medal for all-around gymnastics, bringing the total number of U.S. Olympic gold medals so far to 16.

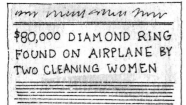

$80,000 DIAMOND RING FOUND ON AIRPLANE BY TWO CLEANING WOMEN

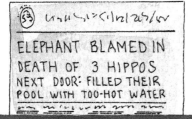

ELEPHANT BLAMED IN DEATH OF 3 HIPPOS NEXT DOOR: FILLED THEIR POOL WITH TOO-HOT WATER

TWO AMTRAK TRAINS COLLIDE IN NEW YORK, IN THE 4th FATAL TRAIN ACCIDENT OF THE MONTH

August

August was named in honor of Roman Emperor Augustus, whose lucky month it was.

BIRTHSTONE *Peridot*

WEDNESDAY
August 1

This week is National Clown Week. Circus Oz, a band of Australian clowns, jugglers, and acrobats, performs at Pepsico's Summerfare '84 in Purchase, New York.

THURSDAY
August 2

At the Olympics in Los Angeles, the U.S. swim team takes 3 more gold medals, and ex-cancer patient Jeffrey Blatnick wins a gold in wrestling.

FRIDAY
August 3

The National Dance Hall of Fame is established, including a National Museum of Dance in Saratoga, New York.

SATURDAY
August 4

A 400-foot-long, 5,900-ton freighter smashes into North America's only living coral reef, about 50 miles south of Miami, Florida.

SUNDAY
August 5

Joan Benoit of Freeport, Maine, wins the first Olympic marathon for women, in a world-record time of 2 hours, 24 minutes, 52 seconds.

MONDAY
August 6

Six members of the environmental activist group Greenpeace climb the Statue of Liberty's scaffolding and unfurl a 30-foot-long banner to protest underground nuclear testing.

TUESDAY
August 7

The snail darter, a small American freshwater fish, is officially off the endangered species list.

WEDNESDAY
August 8

Carl Lewis wins the 200-meter run for his third Olympic gold medal in Los Angeles. • In San Mateo, California, Patrick Galvin and Mark Unger break the hammock-swinging record with a time of 192 hours.

THURSDAY
August 9

MUSEUM BUGGED BY FALSE ALARMS: Spiders spinning webs set off the alarm system four times today, causing the evacuation of the Peabody Museum in Salem, Massachusetts.

WHO ELSE WAS BORN IN AUGUST?
ANNIE OAKLEY

Markswoman, entertainer
She was a member of Buffalo Bill's Wild West
Show, which toured America for 17 years.
BORN August 13, 1860, in Darke County, Ohio

FRIDAY
August 10

People go nuts at the South Carolina Peanut Party in Pelion, South Carolina, with a parade, cooking contest, square dance, and the Peanut Princess pageant!

SATURDAY
August 11

Full Moon

DOLLNAPPING: A Cabbage Patch Kid named Charlotte Luc is reported missing from an apartment in Worcester, Massachusetts. Nothing but the doll was taken.

SUNDAY
August 12

A chicken named Flying Machine flies 83 feet 7 inches to win the International Chicken Flying contest in Brimfield, Illinois.

MONDAY
August 13

The U.S. Postal Service issues a special Smokey the Bear stamp to mark Smokey's 40th anniversary as spokesperson for the National Fire Prevention Program.

TUESDAY
August 14

A two-headed turtle—that also has two sets of lungs—has been found at Jensen Beach, Florida.

WEDNESDAY
August 15

U.S. Olympic medal winners are honored by a ticker-tape parade in New York City. • Two earthquakes rock eastern Iran.

THURSDAY
August 16

HOWLING MAD! Smithtown, New York, has passed a law against any dog barking for more than 15 minutes nonstop.

FRIDAY
August 17

A stamp honoring Roberto Clemente is issued. The outfielder for the Pittsburgh Pirates died in a plane crash while carrying supplies to earthquake victims in Nicaragua in 1972.

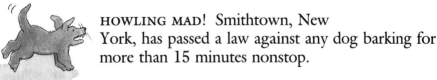

FUN FACT '84

The White House has 132 rooms!

SATURDAY *August 18*	The world's largest pancake is made in High Gate, Vermont—using 2½ tons of Aunt Jemima mix, 1,020 pounds of butter, and 150 pounds of maple syrup—in a 20-foot pan, flipped by a helicopter!
SUNDAY *August 19*	Molasses Reef, the only living coral reef in North America, reopens to recreational divers. There is a 19,000-foot dent—which experts say will last a century—where a freighter recently struck it.
MONDAY *August 20*	The fire department in Madison, Kentucky, responding to an animal distress call, expect to find the usual cat in a tree; instead, the amazed fire fighters find a horse stuck in a well.
TUESDAY *August 21*	In Dagget, California, Solar One, a solar-power plant that cost $141 million, begins full-time production of electricity, generating enough to serve 5,000 people.
WEDNESDAY *August 22*	After a 30-year search, fishermen capture the sea monster that has been living in a lake north of San Francisco, California. It turns out to be a 125-pound white sturgeon.
THURSDAY *August 23*	Timothy Hampson receives the Coast Guard's highest heroism award for fighting off a shark that attacked his fiancée when they were skin diving in the Florida Keys.
FRIDAY *August 24*	Vesuvius Day. This volcano in Italy erupted in A.D. 79, killing 200,000 people and burying the Roman cities of Pompeii and Herculaneum.
SATURDAY *August 25*	Seoul, South Korea, wins the 38th Little League World Series, beating Altamonte Springs, Florida, 6-2, in the final game.
SUNDAY *August 26*	THE ONE THAT GOT AWAY: None of the 4,000 anglers who descend on Long Island Sound today for a fishing contest catch the specially tagged prize bluefish, worth $1 million.
MONDAY *August 27*	Astronomers have new evidence that quasars are actually extremely distant, bright objects that exist near the edge of the universe.

XXIII SUMMER OLYMPICS HIGHLIGHTS

7800 athletes from 140 nations compete in the Summer Olympics in Los Angeles although 14 Communist countries, led by the Soviet Union, do not take part.

- U.S. takes top honors with 174 medals
    Carl Lewis—4 gold medals, track and field
    Valerie Brisco-Hooks—3 gold medals, track and field
    Florence Griffith Joyner—4 medals (3 gold, 1 silver), track and field
    Greg Louganis—2 gold medals, diving
    Mary Lou Retton—5 medals (1 gold, 2 silver, 2 bronze), gymnastics
- Romania comes in second with 53 gold medals
- West Germany places third with a total of 59 medals
- 50,000 people serve as volunteers to help out during the games
- A total of 5,500,000 spectators visit Memorial Coliseum
- 2,500,000,000 people watch on television—80,000,000 people per day
- This is the first time the Olympics are staged without government support

At the closing ceremonies for the 1984 Summer Olympics, 6,000 athletes join in the 3-hour festivities, which include a light show, the landing of a spaceship, and Lionel Richie singing with dozens of break dancers. Good-bye, Olympics XXIII, Hollywood-style!

TUESDAY
August 28

Exactly 80 years ago, the first person ever caught for speeding in an automobile was thrown in jail—for going 20 miles per hour!

WEDNESDAY
August 29

The TSAR (Trans-American Solar-powered Auto Run) reaches its destination in Jacksonville Beach, Florida, becoming the first solar car to cross the country.

THURSDAY
August 30

After 3 delays, space shuttle *Discovery* is finally launched on its very first mission: to deploy three satellites and test a solar sail.

FRIDAY
August 31

JELLYFISH INVASION CLOSES NUCLEAR PLANTS: Two nuclear power plants in Florida are closed because thousands of jellyfish are clogging the water filter system.

CARL LEWIS WINS 4 GOLD MEDALS AT SUMMER OLYMPICS

GREENPEACE MEMBERS CLIMB STATUE OF LIBERTY

SPIDERS SET OFF FALSE ALARM

TWO-HEADED TURTLE DISCOVERED

September

*S*eptember comes from the Latin *septem*, meaning "seven."
This was the seventh month of the old Roman calendar.

BIRTHSTONE *Sapphire*

SATURDAY
September 1

Space shuttle *Discovery* unfolds a 73-by 13-foot solar panel in the first test of its kind in space.

SUNDAY
September 2

Typhoon Ike devastates the Philippines, as winds of 137 miles per hour tear through the country in what meteorologists are calling the worst storm of the century.

MONDAY
September 3

Forty million dollars, the largest lottery jackpot ever won by one person, is claimed today by 28-year-old Mike Wittkowski in Chicago, Illinois.

TUESDAY
September 4

The crew of *Discovery* uses a long robot arm to knock off the troublesome chunk of ice that was stuck to a waste-water vent. All systems are go for landing.

WEDNESDAY
September 5

Be-Late-for-Something Day • Space shuttle *Discovery* lands (on time!) at Edwards Air Force Base after a successful 6-day maiden flight.

THURSDAY
September 6

At the 18th annual Tomato Festival in Reynoldsburg, Ohio, 29-year-old Gary Burkholder is delivering tomatograms as TomatoMan, along with several female Tomato-ettes.

FRIDAY
September 7

More than 100 balloons compete in the Great Reno Balloon Race in Reno, Nevada. • An earthquake hits southern Alaska.

SATURDAY
September 8

American Indian Day • Martina Navratilova beats Chris Evert Lloyd in the U.S. Open women's singles tennis tournament, making the running score between the two competitors 31 victories to 30, in Navratilova's favor.

SUNDAY
September 9

Grandparents' Day • John McEnroe triumphs over Ivan Lendl in the U.S. Open men's singles tennis competition.

SOME ENDANGERED SPECIES IN NORTH AMERICA IN 1984

Mammals   Virginia big-eared bat · Columbian white-tailed deer · San Joaquin kit fox · West Indian manatee · Salt-marsh harvest mouse · Ocelot · Florida panther · Morro Bay kangaroo rat · Delmarva Peninsula fox squirrel · Red wolf

Birds   Masked bobwhite (quail) · California condor · Whooping crane · Eskimo curlew · Bald eagle · American peregrine falcon · Aleutian Canada goose · Brown pelican · Attwater's greater prairie-chicken · Bachman's warbler · Kirtland's warbler · Ivory-billed woodpecker

Reptiles   American alligator · American crocodile

Source: U.S. Fish and Wildlife Service

MONDAY
September 10

Full Moon

The world chess championship match between Anatoly Karpov and Gary Kasparov begins today in Moscow. • In the U.S., teachers are striking in 6 states, giving 140,000 students an extended summer vacation.

TUESDAY
September 11

Scientists report that a diamond has been melted for the first time in history, at Cornell University. The diamond was accidentally melted when a laser was operated at unusually high power. Diamonds are the hardest substance known.

WEDNESDAY
September 12

In Los Angeles, 6,000 immigrants become U.S. citizens. • A baby girl born today in Beaumont, Texas, is named Rhoshandiatellyneshiaunneveshenk Koyaanfsquatsiuty Williams!

THURSDAY
September 13

Hurricane Diana blasts the North Carolina coast with winds of 110 miles per hour before moving out into the Atlantic.

FRIDAY
September 14

Fifty-six-year-old Joe Kittinger takes off from Caribou, Maine, in a 10-story-high helium-filled balloon, hoping to cross the Atlantic.

BACK-TO-SCHOOL NOTES

- There are 43,900,000 elementary and secondary students returning to school this month.
- The average 1984 salary for a teacher in the U.S. is $22,029.

SATURDAY
September 15

The *Saga Siglar*, a replica of a Viking boat built 1,000 years ago, stops in New York City on its way around the world.
• In England, Princess Diana has a second son, Prince Harry.

SUNDAY
September 16

Three bog turtles (*Clemmys muhlenbergii*) have been found in Massachusetts. They are very rare and are usually hard to spot.

MONDAY
September 17

Citizenship Day • In Miami, 10,000 people take the oath of citizenship at the Orange Bowl.

TUESDAY
September 18

Joe Kittinger becomes the first person to cross the Atlantic alone in a balloon when he crash-lands in the mountains in Italy, breaking an ankle. The trip from Maine took 84 hours.

WEDNESDAY
September 19

SNAKE FAKE: A worried zoo-goer calls the Houston Zoo to report that he has not seen the zoo's coral snake move in 9 months. Officials admit the snake is made of rubber!

THURSDAY
September 20

The Philadelphia Zoo announces the healthy birth of Aarthur (who is later renamed Aava), the first of the zoo's aardvark offspring to survive birth. Only 8 zoos in the U.S. house aardvarks.

FRIDAY
September 21

In Shelburne, Vermont, a 5-foot-long boa constrictor has been given anesthesia so it can be removed from the inside of a guitar.

Now this won't hurt a bit.

SATURDAY
September 22

Fall equinox • Comet hunter Tsutomu Seki of Japan becomes the first amateur astronomer to photograph Halley's comet as it speeds toward the sun.

SUNDAY
September 23

Mount Mayan, a volcano in the Philippines, erupts after being dormant for almost 8 years. • Television's Emmy Awards are presented. For dramatic series, Tom Selleck of *Magnum, P.I.* wins best actor and Tyne Daly of *Cagney and Lacey* wins best actress.

FUN FACT '84

Many animals can shed their own limbs when they are injured; spiders will even pull their own legs off.

WHO WAS BORN IN SEPTEMBER?
JIM HENSON

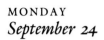

Puppeteer
He created the world-famous Bert, Ernie, Kermit
the Frog, Miss Piggy, and other Muppets featured
on TV and in the movies.
BORN   September 24, 1936, in Greenville,
Mississippi

MONDAY *September 24*	Baseball's Chicago Cubs win their first championship in 39 years when they beat the Pittsburgh Pirates, 4 to 1, for the National League East title.
TUESDAY *September 25*	Billionaire H. Ross Perot announces that he has bought a 687-year-old copy of the Magna Charta, issued on October 12, 1297, by King Edward I. It is an updated version of the 1215 original.

WEDNESDAY
September 26

1,800 Disneyland workers are on strike! There are picket lines outside the park in Anaheim, California. • A sharp earthquake hits San Francisco.

THURSDAY
September 27

First day of Rosh Hashanah • Amateur comet watcher Tsutomu Seki photographs Halley's comet again today.

FRIDAY
September 28

A 52-year-old man is arrested after police find his false teeth (which have his name imprinted on them) in a burglarized apartment in Framingham, Massachusetts.

SATURDAY
September 29

A new Queen Sugar is crowned at the 43d annual Sugar Cane Festival in New Iberia, Louisiana.

SUNDAY
September 30

On this day in 1877, the first U.S. swimming championship was held in the Harlem River in New York.

CHICAGO MAN
WINS $40 MILLION
LOTTERY

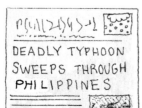

DEADLY TYPHOON
SWEEPS THROUGH
PHILIPPINES

ITALIAN POLICE
ARREST 350
MAFIA MEMBERS

FIRST SOLO
TRANSATLANTIC
BALLOON CROSSING

October

*O*ctober was the eighth month in the old Roman calendar; the name is from the Latin *octo*, meaning "eight."

BIRTHSTONE *Opal*

MONDAY
October 1

The U.S. Postal Service issues a special Family Unity stamp, the first postage stamp designed by a student, Molly LaRue of Shaker Heights High School, Ohio.

TUESDAY
October 2

STRIKE-CALLERS STRIKE: Major league umpires go on strike, demanding more money for umping baseball's upcoming World Series. • Three Soviet cosmonauts return to earth from *Salyut 7* after a record-breaking 237 days in space.

WEDNESDAY
October 3

Richard Miller, an FBI agent, is arrested in San Diego, California, for supplying secret information to the Soviet Union.

THURSDAY
October 4

OPERATION TROPHY KILL: U.S. Fish and Wildlife agents arrest 20 people in 9 states, charging them with killing protected or endangered species.

FRIDAY
October 5

Space shuttle *Challenger* is launched, carrying 5 men and 2 women, the largest crew in the history of space flight. Also on board is the first Canadian astronaut, Marc Garneau.

SATURDAY
October 6

Yom Kippur • Reports show that an increased number of great white sharks have been spotted along California's northern coast.

SUNDAY
October 7

The Statue of Liberty–Ellis Island Foundation announces that the statue's new torch will be made by French artisans using the same process they used to make the original torch. • Baseball's umpires end their strike.

MONDAY
October 8

Columbus Day • The National Zoo in Washington, D.C., has returned 14 zoo-raised golden lion tamarins (rare monkeys known for their beautiful fur) to the wild.

TUESDAY
October 9
Full Moon

In the first game of baseball's World Series, the Detroit Tigers beat the San Diego Padres, 3-2. • Mild earthquake in northwest Georgia.

WHO ELSE WAS BORN IN OCTOBER?
JESSE JACKSON

Civil rights leader, religious leader
He is the founder of Operation Breadbasket and
also of People United to Save Humanity (PUSH)
BORN   October 8, 1941, in Greenville, South
Carolina

OCTOBER IS NATIONAL STAMP COLLECTING MONTH

Stamp collecting is one of the most popular hobbies in the world. People who study and collect stamps are called *philatelists*. The first postage stamps were issued on May 6, 1840, in England—for the amounts of one pence and two pence. Stamp collectors usually search for rare stamps. The harder stamps are to find, the more valuable they are likely to be and the more fun they are to collect.

Besides regular postage stamps, the U.S. Postal Service issues commemorative stamps, which are created to honor an event or a person.

SOME 1984 COMMEMORATIVES

DATE ISSUED	EVENT OR PERSON HONORED		
February 1	Carter G. Woodson, black historian	August 6	Horace Moses, founder of Junior Achievement
February 3	Railroad Caboose (transportation)	August 13	Smokey the Bear
March 25	Founding of Maryland	August 17	Roberto Clemente, baseball player
April 30	Olympic Torch		
May 11	New Orleans World Exposition	September 26	Crime Prevention
June 6	John McCormack, singer	October 1	Family Unity
June 26	St. Lawrence Seaway	October 11	Eleanor Roosevelt, U.S. First Lady
July 13	Roanoke Voyages		

Stamp Collector News   As of August 25, 1984, stamps no longer have on them the letter C, standing for "cents." The last C can be found on a postal card issued September 16.

WEDNESDAY *October 10*	RESCUED: A Cuban freighter picks up two men whose helicopter crashed in the Caribbean Sea while flying to Panama. They had been stranded in a life raft for 36 hours.
THURSDAY *October 11*	Outside the *Challenger*, Kathryn D. Sullivan becomes the second woman in the world to walk in space.

FRIDAY
October 12

The world's southernmost active volcano, Mount Erebus in Antarctica, has erupted with a lava fountain 2,000 feet high.
• A new way of making artificial snow has been invented!

SATURDAY
October 13

Space shuttle *Challenger* makes a perfect landing at Kennedy Space Center in Florida.

SUNDAY
October 14

The Detroit Tigers win the World Series, defeating the San Diego Padres, 8-4, in game 5. It's the Tigers' first World Series victory in 16 years.

MONDAY
October 15

Astronomers have taken the first photograph of what they believe is a solar system being born. It's 50 light-years away.

TUESDAY
October 16

 Dorothy's red slippers (one of several pairs she wore in *The Wizard of Oz*) are stolen from the Humpty-Dumpty and Sons novelty store in San Francisco.

WEDNESDAY
October 17

Disneyland employees return to work in California after a 3-week strike.

THURSDAY
October 18

In Africa, fossil hunters in Kenya find the skull and bones of an unusually large 12-year-old human male from 1,600,000 years ago.

FUN FACT '84

A one-penny British Guiana (now Guyana) stamp sold for $935,000 in 1980.

FRIDAY
October 19

The erupting Mount Erebus causes earthquakes in Antarctica.
• A roller-skating endurance record of 344 hours 18 minutes is set by Isamu Furgen of Japan.

SATURDAY
October 20

A new 177,000-square-foot aquarium opens in Monterey, California. The new Monterey Aquarium cost $40 million to build and is the largest of its kind in the nation.

SUNDAY
October 21

At MetroZoo in Miami, a new exhibit opens: Urban Man, complete with office desk and television set. He is fed his natural diet of hamburgers and french fries to the amusement of onlookers.

MONDAY
October 22

In the Appalachian Mountains of Kentucky, scientists have found the oldest evidence of reptilian life on earth—footprints preserved in a 310,000,000-year-old rock!

TUESDAY *October 23*	Rick Sutcliffe of the Chicago White Sox wins the Cy Young Award for best pitcher in the National League for 1984.
WEDNESDAY *October 24*	In Austin, Texas, Kimberly Coberly sets a new record for using the Hula Hoop: 72 hours.
THURSDAY *October 25*	Ty Techera of Detroit, Michigan, heads out to sea from Newport, Rhode Island, in a 32-foot fiberglass boat for a 27,000-mile solo voyage around the world.
FRIDAY *October 26*	A baby girl receives a baboon's heart in a historic 5-hour transplant operation at Loma Linda University Medical Center in California.
SATURDAY *October 27*	At the Girl Scouts's 43d national convention in Detroit, it is announced that 5-year-olds will be able to join the group for the first time, in a new category that will come before Brownies: the Daisy Girl Scouts.
SUNDAY *October 28*	The New York Marathon is won by Orlando Pizzolato of Italy. Grete Waitz of Norway wins the women's race, for the 6th time in 7 years.
MONDAY *October 29*	The world record for continuous underwater card playing is set by a group of scuba divers who play Uno at the bottom of a Ramada Inn swimming pool for 57 hours in Palm Bay, Florida.
TUESDAY *October 30*	The 1984 Christmas stamp is issued today, created by fourth-grader Danny LaBoccetta of Jamaica, New York. His design was chosen out of 500,000 entries from schoolchildren across the U.S.
WEDNESDAY *October 31*	Halloween • The UNESCO Peace Education Prize of $60,000 is awarded to International Physicians for the Prevention of Nuclear War.

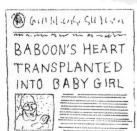

BABOON'S HEART TRANSPLANTED INTO BABY GIRL

PRIME MINISTER INDIRA GHANDI OF INDIA KILLED BY HER BODYGUARDS

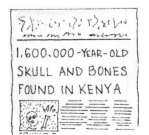

1,600,000-YEAR-OLD SKULL AND BONES FOUND IN KENYA

VOLCANO IN ANTARCTICA ERUPTS

November

November was the ninth month of the old Roman calendar. The name comes from the Latin *novem*, meaning "nine."

BIRTHSTONE *Topaz*

THURSDAY
November 1

Comet Quest, a movie about how to have the best view of Halley's comet in 1986, opens at the National Air and Space Museum in Washington, D.C.

FRIDAY
November 2

NO MORE CANINE CALLUSES: Frank Rotolo of Tucson, Arizona, has invented an elbow pad for dogs!

SATURDAY
November 3

Mild earthquake in southwest Wyoming. • In Key West, Florida, Jerrold Weinstock catches a world-record-breaking cero mackerel that weighs 15 pounds 8 ounces.

SUNDAY
November 4

Coastal engineering researchers in Florida are organizing the nation's first Dial-a-Wave telephone service, a hot line for reporting ocean conditions.

MONDAY
November 5

On this day in 1639, the first post office was established in Massachusetts. • In 1930, the first commercial television broadcast was aired.

TUESDAY
November 6

Election Day. Ronald Reagan and George Bush are reelected as president and vice president of the United States.

WEDNESDAY
November 7

Republican Senator Jake Garn of Utah has been selected to be the first government official to fly in a space shuttle.

THURSDAY
November 8

Full Moon

Space shuttle *Discovery* is launched on a satellite-repair mission from Cape Canaveral, Florida, with a crew of four men and one woman.

FRIDAY
November 9

Joe E. diDonato has been granted a patent for a human-shaped bouncing toy called the Hoppin-Hoppee. • Tornadoes hit Illinois and Missouri.

SATURDAY
November 10

Wild Again wins the horse race with the highest purse in the country, the $3 million Breeders' Cup Classic.

SUNDAY *November 11*	Veteran's Day • Mark Roberts wins the Cal-Ca-Chew jambalaya eating contest in Lake Charles, Louisiana, by gulping down a pint in 1 minute 45 seconds.
MONDAY *November 12*	The world's first salvage operation in space is performed. Two astronauts from the *Discovery* retrieve a nonfunctioning satellite and bring it back into the cargo bay of the spacecraft.
TUESDAY *November 13*	Ryne Sandberg, second baseman for the Chicago Cubs, is named Most Valuable Player of 1984 in the National League.
WEDNESDAY *November 14*	A painting by Italian artist Amedeo Modigliani is sold for $4.62 million, the highest price ever paid for one of his works. • The third-largest blue diamond in the world is sold at Christie's in Switzerland for $4.6 million.
THURSDAY *November 15*	THE CABBAGE RUSH: There's already a line outside Babyland General Hospital in Cleveland, Georgia, to get Cabbage Patch dolls for Christmas!

ELECTION FACTS AND FIGURES

- 92,653,000 Americans voted, only 53 percent of eligible voters in the nation.
- Electoral vote: Reagan—525 • Popular vote: Reagan—54,281,858
  Mondale—13   Mondale—37,457,215
- 136 people officially declared that they were running for president.
- In 1984, Ronald Reagan (age 73) was the oldest man ever to be elected president of the United States. The average age for presidents is 55.

FRIDAY *November 16*	The space shuttle *Discovery* returns to Cape Canaveral after a successful 8-day rescue mission. Two satellites have been brought back to earth.
SATURDAY *November 17*	NASA technicians begin preparing *Discovery* for a top-secret mission scheduled for January 1985.
SUNDAY *November 18*	For only the second time in 100 years, the American Kennel Club stages a show. With 8,075 dogs entered, it is the largest dog show ever held in North America. Top winner: a German shepherd named Ch. Covy Tucker Hills Manhattan.

MONDAY *November 19*	Anniversary of Abraham Lincoln's famous Gettysburg address in 1863 • On this day in 1969, the *Apollo 12* lunar module landed on the moon, and astronauts Charles Conrad, Jr., and Alan L. Bean walked on the moon.
TUESDAY *November 20*	Mr. Rogers donates one of the familiar sweaters he wears on "Mr. Rogers' Neighborhood" to the Smithsonian Institution in a ceremony at the Museum of American History in Washington, D.C. It was handmade by his mother.
WEDNESDAY *November 21*	Plans are under way for a sea voyage by a replica of the *Godspeed*, one of the 3 ships that crossed the Atlantic in 1607 (13 years before the *Mayflower*) with the founders of Jamestown, Virginia.
THURSDAY *November 22*	Thanksgiving. Macy's 58th annual Thanksgiving Day Parade in New York City features a 60-foot Donald Duck in honor of his 50th birthday this year. • A 1707 Stradivarius violin is sold at Sotheby's in London for a record $491,040.

FUN FACT '84

President James Garfield could write with both his hands at the same time. He could also write in Latin with one hand and in Greek with the other!

FRIDAY *November 23*	A strong earthquake, measuring 5.7 on the Richter scale, shakes a wide area of central California and western Nevada and causes dangerous rock slides. There are also several hundred aftershocks.
SATURDAY *November 24*	For 5 hours, 380 skiers are stranded between 40 and 200 feet in the air when a ski lift breaks down on Mount Pluto in Truckee, California. • Today is the 110th anniversary of the invention of barbed wire.
SUNDAY *November 25*	William J. Schroeder of Jasper, Indiana, becomes the second person in history to receive a permanent artificial heart.
MONDAY *November 26*	An earthquake beneath the Sierra Nevada shakes Mammoth Mountain in California.

WHO ELSE WAS BORN IN NOVEMBER?
JAMES GARFIELD

Twentieth president of the United States
After serving as a Republican congressman from 1863 to 1880, he was inaugurated as president in 1881 and was assassinated later that year. He was the 2d U.S. president to be assassinated in office.
BORN November 19, 1831, in Cuyahoga County, Ohio

TUESDAY
November 27

MISSING LINK? Researchers at Florida State University are studying a strange species of blind shrimp they have discovered in parts of Bermuda and Hawaii—the only shrimps ever found that have no claws.

WEDNESDAY
November 28

McDonald's has sold its 50 *billionth* hamburger. In 1984, the fast-food chain sells approximately 140 burgers every second!

THURSDAY
November 29

Navy demolition experts blow up an errant torpedo by remote control after it is accidentally snared by a fishing boat in Rhode Island Sound. Officials believe it to be an old World War II test-warhead.

FRIDAY
November 30

The first volume of the first Sumerian dictionary (the world's first written language!) is published by the University of Pennsylvania Press.

—How 'bout that, Ron?

PRESIDENTIAL ELECTION BOX

Republican President Ronald Reagan and Vice President George Bush were reelected—in a record-breaking landslide—to a second term in the White House on November 6, 1984. Ronald Reagan won in 49 states. The Democratic candidates were former Vice President Walter Mondale and Representative Geraldine Ferraro, the first woman candidate for vice president.

380 SKIERS STRANDED ON SKI LIFT

PRESIDENT REAGAN REELECTED IN A LANDSLIDE

SECOND MAN IN HISTORY GETS ARTIFICIAL HEART

MR. ROGERS DONATES SWEATER TO MUSEUM

December

December used to be the tenth month of the year (the Latin *decem* means "ten"). The old Roman calendar began with March.

BIRTHSTONE *Turquoise*

SATURDAY
December 1

Tickets go on sale in Atlanta for a Prince concert, and fans break 4 plate-glass windows as they push to get tickets. 34,000 seats are sold in the first 2 hours!

SUNDAY
December 2

The puffin, a northern seabird with a yellow, red, and blue beak, is reappearing in numbers in Maine after a 3-year effort by conservationists to save the species.

MONDAY
December 3

A white rhinoceros named Zimba is born at the London Zoo in England.

TUESDAY
December 4

The National Geographic Society reports the recovery of a fabulous treasure that includes gold ingots, medallions, beads, and pottery from the oldest shipwreck ever found. The ship sank 3,400 years ago off the coast of Turkey.

WEDNESDAY
December 5

Hawaii has voted in the humuhumu-nukunuku-a-puala as the official state fish.

THURSDAY
December 6

The FBI seizes more than 5,000 fake Cabbage Patch Kids from a warehouse near Detroit. The phony dolls have been turning up all over the country—with a peculiar odor!

FRIDAY
December 7

A hundred people play the parts of Christmas ornaments on a 30-foot tree, creating the 30th annual Singing Christmas Tree in Charlotte, North Carolina.

SATURDAY
December 8

Full Moon

Baffled scientists today say they have no idea what caused a loud roar and vibrations that shook buildings yesterday throughout San Diego and Orange County in California.

FUN FACT '84

The katydid hears through holes in its legs.

SUNDAY
December 9

President and Mrs. Reagan return from Camp David with their new dog, Lucky. They received the 9-week-old sheepdog from 6-year-old Kristen Ellis, the March of Dimes Poster Child.

MONDAY
December 10

Human Rights Day • In Oslo, Norway, South African Bishop Desmond Tutu receives the Nobel Peace Prize for his nonviolent struggle against apartheid. The ceremony is temporarily interrupted by a bomb scare.

TUESDAY
December 11

Astronomers report the sighting of what is perhaps the first planet ever found outside our Solar System. It's about the size of Jupiter and orbits a star approximately 21 light-years from Earth.

WEDNESDAY
December 12

Archaeologists in Florida find 7,000-year-old human skulls buried in peat at the bottom of a lake and are amazed to discover that the brains are still intact!

TOY BOX '84
America's Top Playthings

Preemie	Lurky	Cabbage Patch Kid	He Man and the
Koosa	Stripe	Optimus Prime	Masters of the Universe
GoBots	Montgomery	The Bear Boom	
Crack-ups	Elvis Bearsley	Muffy Vanderbear	
Hero Jr.	My Little Pony	Care Bear Wish Bear	

THURSDAY
December 13

A "dark sky" ordinance is passed in San Diego County limiting the use of electric lights at night so that astronomers will have a better view of the night sky.

FRIDAY
December 14

The U.S. Navy bans beards on sailors. All chin growth, which has been allowed since the 1970s, is now forbidden.

SATURDAY
December 15

Soviet spacecraft *Vega I* takes off on its mission to rendezvous with Halley's comet in March 1986. An American comet-dust detector is on board.

SUNDAY
December 16

The Carnegie Foundation awards 21 medals for heroism, including one to Reverend John J. Sholly, who leapt into a freezing Iowa river to save a 78-year-old man from drowning.

MONDAY *December 17*	Wright Brothers Day, the anniversary of the famous first flight at Kitty Hawk, North Carolina, in 1903
TUESDAY *December 18*	The traditional Christmas cards of Elaine, Arkansas—wooden ones 4 feet by 8 feet—are propped along the state highway. This year there are 32; the town adds one every year.
WEDNESDAY *December 19*	Hanukkah begins at sunset. • An extremely rare parrot from Borneo has been stolen from a zoo in Poland. It is the only one of its kind in the country.
THURSDAY *December 20*	AT&T Bell Laboratories announces the development of a new computer memory chip—the Megabit—that can store more than a million bits of electronic memory.
FRIDAY *December 21*	Winter solstice, the shortest day of the year. • The Soviets launch *Vega II* on their second spacecraft mission to Halley's comet.

THE CABBAGE PATCH SCAM

Hundreds of people were surprised and disappointed when they answered a nationwide advertisement that read: "Send $34.95, and we will send you a Cabbage Patch." That is just what customers got—a packet of seeds to grow cabbages in a garden!

SATURDAY *December 22*	The world chess championship match between Anatoly Karpov and Gary Kasparov continues in Moscow. After 34 games and 102 days, it is now the longest world chess match on record!
SUNDAY *December 23*	The movie *Ghostbusters*, which opened June 8, has pulled in more than $200 million at the box office. *Ghostbusters* lunch boxes, toys, and T-shirts are hot sellers this Christmas.
MONDAY *December 24*	Christmas Eve • A high-ranking Soviet physicist, Vladimirovich Kulikov, defects in Chicago.
TUESDAY *December 25*	Christmas • Swarms of jellyfish sting more than 1,500 bathers in south Florida.
WEDNESDAY *December 26*	A strange noise coming from a suitcase causes authorities to evacuate the Lafayette, Louisiana, airport. A bomb squad tracks down the noise to a battery-operated Zoid toy robot!

WHO ELSE WAS BORN IN DECEMBER?
WALT DISNEY

Cartoonist, producer, founder of Disneyland
The creator of Mickey Mouse, he was a pioneer in
cartoon animation.
BORN   December 5, 1901, in Chicago, Illinois

THURSDAY
December 27

A man-made comet is launched from a satellite 60,000 miles above the Pacific Ocean. The comet produces a tail 10,000 miles long.

FRIDAY
December 28

The numbers are in: More than 20,000,000 Cabbage Patch dolls have made their way into homes throughout the U.S.

SATURDAY
December 29

The Smithsonian Institution reports the discovery of a new type of underwater plant life (a purple alga) that grows deeper and with less light than anything ever seen before!

SUNDAY
December 30

A plaque in honor of George Orwell, who wrote the famous novel *1984*, is unveiled in the apartment where he lived in London, England. *1984*, written in 1949, was a best-seller this year in America.

MONDAY
December 31

New Year's Eve • Anatoly Karpov and Gary Kasparov are *still* vying for the world chess championship in Moscow. They are in their 37th game now, after finally agreeing to call the 36th a draw.

THE LATEST ROBOT FIGURES

In 1984, after almost 200 years of counting people, the U.S. Bureau of the Census counted the annual production of robots in America for the first time. The results: 5,535 new robots in the U.S.!

3,400-YEAR-OLD ARTIFACTS ARE RECOVERED FROM BRONZE-AGE SHIPWRECK OFF COAST OF TURKEY

SCIENTISTS DISCOVER FIRST PLANET OUTSIDE SOLAR SYSTEM

OLDEST GORILLA IN CAPTIVITY DIES AT AGE 54

FIRST ARTIFICIAL COMET LAUNCHED

YOUR YEAR AT A GLANCE

A lot happened the year you were born. How many events shown on the cover can you identify? Turn the page upside down for the answers.

1. Bald Eagle Alert (See January) 2. Hawaii's Mauna Loa erupts (March 25) 3. The Washington Monument turns 100 (See January) 4. Ten-thousand starlings settle in Fairfield, California (January 8) 5. Rattlesnake Rodeo held in Opp, Alabama (March 2) 6. Trans-Atlantic single-handed yacht race (June 2) 7. The first fully portable cellular phone is introduced to the public (March 13) 8. Weird Harold wins Calaveras County Jumping Frog Contest (May 21) 9. International Festival of the Magical Arts, Scottsdale, Arizona (January 21) 10. Detroit Tigers win World Series (October 14) 11. 100th anniversary of first American roller coaster (June 16) 12. Dorothy's red slippers (from *The Wizard of Oz*) stolen (October 16) 13. Baby aardvark born at Philadelphia Zoo (September 20) 14. Mondale chooses Ferraro as his running mate (July 12) 15. Olympic Summer Games torch lit (May 7) 16. French daredevils parachute off the Eiffel Tower (April 18) 17. First unattached space walk in history (February 7)